Regulate me now

Danie Harris

Dedication

For my darling girl who inspires me every day.

Here are those strategies and soothers I often share with you. I can not wait until you become a black belt reregulation champion, Bold and Fiercely Thriving in the large or quiet Life you Choose and Create with Love always Xx

To all of you wondrous people who need to reregulate your nervous system now. You've got this!

Safety Notice

Your safety is the top priority if you are in immediate danger or facing a threatening situation.

If possible, remove yourself from the dangerous situation. Seek a safe location, such as a public place or a trusted friend's home.

Contact Emergency Services for your region right away.

If you cannot leave or feel unsafe making a call, consider reaching out to someone you trust who can help you get to safety.

If you feel unsafe at any time, please take the best action to protect you.

Contents

How to use this book

Welcome to Regulate Me Now, a guide
for immediate care with intense overwhelm, anxiety or dysregulation.

Provided are prompts and techniques to help you reregulate. A flexible resource where information is repeated and spaced creatively to accommodate different kinds of readers. Please turn to the pages that serve you best at any given moment.

We want your body and mind to find the calm and the power of self-agency to live your life with more intention, joy, and ease.

Every day brings new challenges. Please see them as opportunities to understand yourself more deeply. Keeping in mind that resistance is a natural biological response, allow yourself to be open to trying new approaches in a learner mode. Get curious about yourself and your experiences with dysregulation. Neuroscience widely acknowledges that your incredible brain can change through simple mindfulness practices.

Be proactive, patient, and gentle with yourself as you work through these actions. It's essential to put yourself first. If any part of this book feels difficult, ask: How can I make this easy or less stressful or fun? Embrace your reactions, even if they seem cheesy - they're clues to areas that need attention for your betterment.

It is your life to live, why not live it well!

The Author's Story

For most of my life, dysregulation ranging from mild to extreme has persistently consumed me, making my earlier life exhausting.

Reason for this book - I've faced a truckload of health issues covering five decades with very little support. Misdiagnosed in my early 30s with depression, I was blacking out and unable to stand up. With no choice, no shame, I would crawl into the doctors' offices. Hours away from death's door, endocrinologists of all stages came to gawk at this rare event: Me, in intensive care with Addison's Disease - a condition that requires constant stress level regulation due to the inability to produce cortisol.

For a year before the diagnosis, my symptoms were dismissed as psychological while I physically deteriorated. I mention this as dysregulation is often viewed only as a psychological or emotional issue, "Just get over it," a pat-pat on the back and an antidepressant prescription.

For some of us, emotional dysregulation arises with neurological dysregulation. Understanding this distinction can take the pressure off, especially for those who identify as codependents, that our parents and we are not to blame, it is not our fault.

Published in 2024, I read an article mocking nervous system regulation as a fad, but I know firsthand how essential this work is. Dysregulation can lead to severe health problems and leave us unable to function. Online life coaches looking for answers for their own recovery, like Richard Grannon and Anna Runkle, from Crappy Childhood Fairy, helped me understand and navigate my Complex PTSD and codependent tendencies with humor and clarity, which has positively changed my life.

It's not about quick fixes or social media trends. Breakthroughs happen with accumulated knowledge, meaningful intent, and daily practices.

My game-changer? On top of a new self-care routine, in a 30 day challenge created by Richard Grannon, I spent a half-day of intensive, self-directed visualization exploring my future self that I embodied into the present continuum. Everything lifted and shifted — confidence, inner calm, seeing clear boundaries for the first time, easy decision-making, self-agency, self-advocacy, no body pain, no numbing, no tingling, and that uncomfortable sensation of nerves being twisted up in the body, no muscle fatigue, no physical rigidity, no clawed hand and arm, less critical talk, less negative tunneling, stopped over-sharing (well, half of it), lighter in spirit, enthusiastic about pursuing more of everything, dreaming bigger, lost the overwhelming sense of fear, whoophh, less hypervigilance, less avoidance, no general anxiety, detached from people pleasing and the needs of others before mine, easily implementing self-care, and less attachment, more space to just be. I catch myself smiling in the middle of the day while doing ordinary tasks, and every time I remember that particular visualization, waves full of gratitude open me up to discover (something that made me cringe and alluded me) .... self Love!

I'm not a doctor; I'm a visual artist, researcher, and lover of slower living. I embrace my dyslexic ways and CPTSD outcomes for their potential gold. Through my long and windy life of health issues, this little guide is the grateful outcome of my experiences, years of researching the many evidence-based studies, and a multitude of support from professionals and online coaches who have shaped the content of these pages.

I'm here to share what I've learned and to help, Regulate you now. xx

What does intense triggering look like for you?

For many, it's that rising tension that starts with something small like a missed deadline, a minor disagreement with someone, or even a simple change in plans.

Even when you tell yourself, "It's not a big deal," it still feels like everything is spiraling out of control, your chest tightening, your mind racing, and you say things you regret and don't even mean. On high alert, the smallest sensations are amplified, sounds are louder, and every light brighter. Your thoughts become rapid and disjointed, replaying past events or imagining worst-case scenarios. Trapped in a loop of distress, everything around you fades, and all you can focus on is the intensity of the feelings flooding your system. Or you freeze up or zone out and can't focus for days. It's a full-body, full-mind experience that demands attention, leaving you struggling to return to the present moment. It's like being caught in a storm where all you can do is wait it out.

You are dysregulated

Reregulating the nervous system means calming or resetting the nervous system after it has been thrown off balance, often due to stress, trauma, or anxiety.

Regulate yourself now

When dysregulating. Sit with it and Acknowledge

It's intense and overwhelming. Sometimes it feels like it might never end

In the midst of this intense wave, know that your experience – the flooding of emotions, sensations, and racing mind – is valid and real

It is your body's way of signaling that something important is happening within

This can happen when you are in a safe situation - you have been triggered, although there is no immediate threat

It's okay to feel this deeply   you are safe

Remember it does not define you. It is an experience you are having

As you navigate through it, remember that these sensations, although powerful, will pass

You are not alone

There is great power in acknowledging and gently sitting with it

Allow yourself the grace to move through it at your
own pace

knowing that you have the capacity to find calm on
the other side

Say this gently to yourself (if not alone)
Say this softly out loud while stroking your arms:

I am dysregulating right now and that is ok

I am ok. Although I am dysregulating right now

I am safe

Repeat

If it is easier, repeat over:

I am safe

Simplify where you can, and remind yourself that
there's room for calm even in chaos. You're doing the
best you can, and that's enough.

Nervous System Dysregulation Impacts

Affecting cognitive, emotional, and sensory processes

Dysregulation affects everyone at some point and is temporary and manageable.

Exposure to chronic stress and trauma, as well as underlying health issues like anxiety, can lead to persistent dysregulation, impacting overall health.

When the body's ability to maintain balance is compromised and continuously out of balance, it can lead to chronic health issues such as cardiovascular diseases, metabolic conditions like diabetes, gastrointestinal disorders, worsening of inflammatory conditions, and so much more.

Some Types of Dysregulation

Autonomic Nervous System,

Mood - anxiety, depression,

Autism, Insomnia, Dyslexia,

Post-Traumatic Stress Disorder PTSD,

Complex PTSD/ complex trauma,

Attention Deficit Hyperactivity Disorder ADHD,

Alzheimer's Disease, Fibromyalgia, Epilepsy,

Autoimmune Diseases, Parkinson's Disease,

Obsessive-Compulsive Disorder OCD

Signs and Symptoms

Circle or add yours

Cognitive

inability to 'think straight' and maintain focus

difficult to control the language used and tone of voice

making quick, irrational decisions

flooding thoughts

confusion

rumination

loop thinking

excessive worrying

racing mind

a loud inner critic voice

A loud outer critic voice

negative self-talk

disconnection

Emotions

discombobulated

a feeling of great fear, doom

a feeling to immediately escape

overpowered by anger, sadness

a quick switch of mood

continuous crying

feeling helpless

feeling out of control

deep sense of depletion

difficulty in shifting negative emotions

difficulty in connecting with feelings

irritability

feeling left out

feeling fragile or little

everything feels too hard

Physical

difficult to breath

shakiness

racing heart

easily startled

sweating

dry mouth

headaches

numbing

tingling

pain

nausea

muscle tension

muscle fatigue

stomach in knots

inflammation

blank face

dizziness

feeling faint

chest tightness

loss of appetite

sleep disturbances

autoimmune function

tinnitus increases in volume

heightened sensitivity to stimuli

Stress and Our Biology

Our wondrous and complex body systems manage stress and maintain balance.

A nonstop nervous system that continuously takes in information from your surrounding environment and sends it to other systems, coordinating movement, sensory perception, and cognitive processes, all while maintaining our internal balance.

The Brain

Amygdala Plays a crucial role in processing emotions, especially fear and anxiety. The brain's alarm system detects threats and activates the stress response by signaling the hypothalamus to initiate immediate fight, flight or freeze actions to keep you safe.

Prefrontal Cortex Responsible for decision-making, impulse control, and rational thinking. It helps regulate the amygdala's stress response through its conscious thoughts and reasoning. Under stress, it shrinks, leading to impulsive or irrational actions.

The Autonomic Nervous System (ANS)

Sympathetic Nervous System (SNS) Prepares the body for the "fight or flight" response. It mobilizes the body's resources in response to stress, increasing heart rate, blood pressure, and blood flow to muscles while shutting down non-essential functions like digestion.

Parasympathetic Nervous System (PNS)
Responsible for the "rest and digest" state. It calms you down after a stressful event, bringing your body back to a state of balance.

Endocrine System

HPA Axis - Hypothalamus Pituitary Adrenal Axis
Involves interactions between the hypothalamus, pituitary gland, and adrenal glands. Controls the release of cortisol, the primary stress hormone.

The Neurotransmitter System

Cortisol maintains blood sugar levels, metabolism, and inflammation control and supports the body's circadian rhythm. Released during stress, it helps the body manage immediate threats but can be harmful if levels remain elevated.

Adrenaline (epinephrine) and noradrenaline (norepinephrine) manage functions like heart rate, blood pressure and the "fight or flight" response.

Serotonin affects mood, sleep, appetite, and digestion.

Dopamine regulates mood, motivation, reward, and motor control.

Oxytocin involves bonding, social interaction, reproductive functions, and reduction of stress.

Endorphins act as natural painkillers and are involved in pleasure and pain relief.

GABA (gamma-aminobutyric acid) is the primary inhibitory neurotransmitter promoting relaxation and balance.

Trauma, Chronic Stress and Dysregulation

Under normal circumstances, the SNS and PNS work harmoniously to maintain equilibrium. When something goes wrong, this balance is lost.

With prolonged stress, the hypothalamus can signal a continuous release of the stress hormones, keeping the body in a state of heightened alert. Excessive cortisol shrinks the prefrontal cortex, blocking clear thinking and impulse control. Simultaneously, the amygdala becomes overactive, stuck in hypervigilance, heightening anxiety and emotional reactivity, signaling danger even when it's not present. The hippocampus shrinks, struggling to process new memories and learned information and increasing the susceptibility to depression.

Our Beautiful Brain
and the Transformative Power
of Plasticity

The brain's remarkable neuroplasticity is its ability to adapt and form new neural connections in response to learning, experience, or injury. Using Functional Magnetic Resonance Imaging (fMRI) neuroscientists can observe this process.

Neuroplasticity empowers the brain to replace harmful circuits formed during trauma with healthier patterns. This involves boosting synaptic strength, creating new ones, and generating new neurons. Consistent practice of stress-reducing techniques,

e.g., mindfulness meditation enables the brain to reshape stress responses formed over years of trauma. Many scientific studies have revealed significant results regardless of practitioners' experience and age. By deliberately focusing attention and embracing discomfort, we can create new neuron pathways that reinforce new patterns of positive perception.

It's a winning story!

Containment Method

Set aside overwhelming emotions so you can function better in the moment. The idea is to revisit them when you are more equipped to handle them.

1. Identify the overwhelm: recognize the emotions or thoughts.

2. Create a safe space: visualize a comfortable place where you can mentally get calm. It could be a real place or an imagined location that feels peaceful.

3. Visualize a containment box: imagine a container you can securely close and where you can temporarily put your overwhelming thoughts, feelings, or memories.

4. Placing the emotions inside: picture yourself taking the overwhelming emotions or thoughts and letting them flow into this box.

5. Close and lock the box: visualize closing and locking it all inside.

6. Store the box: imagine placing the box in a safe location until you're ready to deal with the contents.

7. Return to the present: gently bring your attention to your breath or to your surroundings.

This version from Therapy in a Nutshell by a licensed therapist, Emma McAdam

Nervous system dysregulation

Is an imbalance or malfunction in the nervous system that disrupts its normal functions and responses to internal and external stimuli, increasing the sensitivity to stress.

Many people live with a dysregulated nervous system for long periods without knowing it.

A dysregulated nervous system is not so flexible at returning from an intense stress response to the baseline state of calm and balance. Instead of quickly rebounding, you might find yourself stuck in heightened states of anxiety or a prolonged period of exhaustion, making it harder to manage daily challenges.

It can contribute to developing new or exacerbating preexisting chronic conditions.

Some Causes

Chronic stress, trauma, genetics, environmental factors like lack of sleep or sleep disorders, social isolation, toxins, nutritional deficiencies, substance abuse, autoimmune conditions, hormonal imbalances like menopause, chronic pain, infections, inflammation, and sensory overloading can all contribute, result or worsen dysregulation!

Triggers

Are stressors or events that provoke a strong physiological and emotional response. Behaviorally, they can evoke impulsive, defensive reactions in ways that are disproportionate to the current situation.

Triggers are as diverse as people.

Some everyday things can trigger your nervous system into an overactive state and undermine where and what you are presently doing. They may be related to specific smells, sights, or receiving critical feedback: a stranger's flip comment, your partner being quiet, someone not texting, or even by rushing around.

If you have a feeling of urgency, this is a clue that you are triggered.

Some common types
Sensory

Loud or sudden noises, specific smells (like perfume, smoke, certain foods)

Certain lighting (flashing or flickering lights)

Emotional

Feelings of rejection or abandonment (a friend cancels plans)

Criticism, negative feedback or perceived failure

Sudden changes in mood (someone's tone of voice or facial expression)

Social

Arguments, conflicts with others

Feeling left out or ignored in social settings

Witnessing someone being mistreated

Physical

Illness, pain, injury, medical settings or procedures

Fatigue, lack of sleep

Physical contact or touch, especially if unexpected

Situational

Being in crowded places, confined spaces (lack of personal space)

Involving authority figures, power dynamics (a stern look)

Specific locations (like hospitals or schools)

Cognitive

Intrusive thoughts, memories

Hearing others' trauma stories

Overthinking, excessive worrying

High expectations, toxic self talk

Relational

Relationships that mimic past abusive dynamics

Dependency on others for emotional support

Trust issues in close relationships

Life Changes

Getting married, relationship break ups, having a baby, moving homes, loss of work, losing a loved one

Fight Flight Freeze Fawn

Are instinctive survival strategies our nervous system uses in response to danger. When dysregulated, these strategies become overactive or are triggered inappropriately, leading to a default reaction disproportionate to the actual threat or stressor.

Fight responding with anger or aggression to a perceived threat.

Flight manifests as chronic avoidance or anxiety to escaping situations.

Freeze may cause a person to shut down, feel paralyzed, unable to make decisions or take action, reflecting a deep sense of helplessness.

Fawn (relational) often appears as excessive people-pleasing or difficulty asserting oneself, a learned strategy to prevent conflict and maintain safety.

Be here to regulate now

Generously be kind to yourself

These are suggestions only. If they do not feel right then it's not right for you now.
And that is ok.

Excuse yourself from others and go somewhere safe.
Remove yourself from the trigger and further reactivity

Splash cold water on your face and enjoy the drying

Lather up your hands and rinse under warm water
Focus on how soothing every step feels when washing your hands

EFT - Tapping

Tapping your fingers on the side of your other hand
and together speak your experience:
Although I feel my heart and mind racing, I am safe
Although I feel dysregulated, it is ok, I am safe
Although I have feelings of anger, it is ok, I am safe
These feelings are not dangerous and will pass

SHAKE your hands
Bounce about
Jiggle out your whole body
Squeeze your arms or pat them up,
include deep breaths in and longer ones out

Go for a walk and focus on the nature around you
333: Seek out 3 things to closely observe, listen to 3
things, move 3 different parts of your body

I am safe   I am safe   I am safe

I am safe   I am safe   I am safe

I am safe   I am safe   I am safe

This feeling is a feeling

and I am safe

This feeling will pass

Space

Create a physical space, like a cozy room or a mental place you can imagine when you need comfort.
When you are safe, your whole system will act accordingly.

Boundaries

Setting boundaries means protecting your energy, saying no, and avoiding overwhelming situations. Prioritize yourself - no matter how demanding others are with you, communicate your limits. Boundaries aren't about pushing people away; they're about creating a safe space where you can thrive, and by respecting your own needs, you invite others to do the same.

Feeling Safe in Body

Emotions are valid, even the difficult ones.

When you are activated, try to be still

Try, patience, self-compassion

Stick with it for 1 min, next time 2 mins …

Get used to your scary, uncomfortable feelings.

Prepare to suck at it… and if you hate doing it, that's ok.. try to push through and try again.

Creating flexibility requires ongoing attention and care to build trust

And keep plenty of tricks up your sleeve.

Mindful Awareness and Body

Mindfulness practices are plentiful and incredibly beneficial, even for just 2 minutes per day.

Take action to move back into your present body.

Check-in with a Body Scan

Stay tuned into your body's sensations without judgment. Regularly check for changes like a racing heart, shallow breathing, muscle tension, or heat rising in your body. Bring your attention to take prompt action to reregulate.

Progressive Muscle Relaxation (PMR)

Start from your feet and work up to the head, systematically tensing each muscle for a few seconds, then slowly relax them.

Target an area like shoulders, hands or face when out and about.

Shake out and swing, playful dance to stretches, all will loosen up any rigidity.

Mindful Movement

Gentle movement with awareness like yoga, tai chi, or qigong connects the mind and body beautifully, maintaining flexibility and balance to develop a sense of agency over your physical experience.

Grounding Techniques

Focus on connecting with the present moment by feeling the sensations of your feet on the ground, touching different textures, observing up and close your surroundings, or using grounding affirmations:

"I am present and fully engaged with the world around me."

"My breath anchors me in the present."

Self-Massage

Gently massage areas of tension or discomfort. Hands, feet, neck, and head are all good places to target. When out, hand massaging is discreet.

Mindfulness Meditation

This practice is essential to maintain regulation and to create those new neural pathways we need. Focus on your breath, sensations, or a visual anchor point in your surroundings to bring your attention back to the present without any judgment. It keeps you present, grows your mental muscles, allows in space.

Visualization

Imagine a calming and safe place. Use guided imagery or visualization to create a mental image that promotes relaxation and positive emotions. This might involve imagining a peaceful place or envisioning a positive outcome. I picture each cell in my body smiling or the air I breathe flooding me with smiling life.

Mindful Tasking

Go clean, sweep, or do some weeding mindfully. As you weed, feel the soil, notice the resistance of each root, and sync your movements with your breath. Go into flow by letting yourself get lost in the rhythm of repetition. When thoughts enter, notice they are thoughts and then gently bring your focus back to the task.

Temperature Regulation

Use temperature-related strategies like taking a warm bath or shower to relax muscles or cold water to interrupt the dysregulation.

Sensory Regulation

Carry a tactile thing like a smooth stone or hand cream to soothe. Reduce the sensory overload with noise-canceling headsets, wear sunglasses, choose quieter venues like a smaller grocery store and times when people frequent less, rest up before facing highly stimulated situations, use guided meditations, declutter your home or workspace.

Time in Nature

Spend time in natural surroundings or nurture a pot plant. Walking in a park, soaking up some sun while resting on a lawn, and feeling the grass between your toes and fingers helps us connect and soothe.

Mindful check-in

Notice negative thought patterns, become aware of catastrophic thinking (expecting the worst-case scenario) or a sudden increase in self-critical or blaming thoughts.

These may be followed by a strong emotional response in you.

How are you feeling? Name 3 feelings; once acknowledged acceptance can move in.

Using an online Emotion Wheel is helpful.

Dysregulation Intensity Scale

Rate your dysregulation on a scale from 1 to 10, where 1 is completely calm and 10 is the worst. Do this anytime throughout the day when you notice your nervous system is activated or emotionally reactive. Rate your level again after any action to interrupt or soothe your current state.

This can be an incredible tool for receiving that lovely dopamine hit when you recognize and acknowledge the levels lowering toward calm.

Daily Self Care Plan

Prioritize daily habits to cultivate structure, stability, and self-agency.

Sleep: Aim for 7.5 hours by sticking to a consistent bedtime 10 pm and a consistent wake time, including weekends. Create a restful sleep environment—dark, quiet, cool—and keep phones out of the bedroom. Step outside after waking to assist your circadian rhythm

Exercise: Incorporating gentle movements like yoga, tai chi, Qigong, or stretching, are beautiful ways to connect the mind and body and keep you moving. Refresh your attention and engage your senses by going for an afternoon walk.

Good Food: Focus on fiber-rich whole foods, protein, and healthy fats. Avoid processed and sugary foods that disrupt your body's balance with sugar spikes. Stay hydrated.

Mindfulness: Add your favorite soothers and reregulate exercises, practicing on-call-ready to buffer against stress and dysregulation.

Play and Gratitude: Enjoy, laugh, and play, such as bird watching, kayaking, Vicar of Dibley reruns, and self-massages. Welcome in and grow gratitude!

Some days may require more focus on one area to maintain balance and adapt as needed.

Consistently caring for you is a daily reminder of you loving you.

Emotional Flooding and Emotional Flashbacks

Emotional Flooding is the overwhelming experience of intense emotions, like fear and anger, in response to a stressful situation. You go offline, and physiological responses are heightened, making it challenging to stay calm or rational.

Emotional flashbacks are sudden and intense experiences common in people with Complex PTSD. They are subtle, can last for long periods, and it's like reliving past trauma without recalling specific memories.

Trauma-related dysregulation can distort your ability to process thoughts and emotions, making you overly focused on others' perceptions of you.

Unresolved trauma can lead to projecting your wounds onto others.

Recognize that this is a distraction that keeps you stuck.

A Self Compassion Reframe Exercise

Recognize when you blame or criticize yourself or others. When you see it, choose kindness by replacing it with gratitude thoughts. Say it out loud and actively bring in the feeling of joy; use visualization if it helps.

Or name 5 personal strengths and your top 5 Core Values.

The Daily Practice
of resentment and fear release

Writing down any thoughts and feelings of resentment and fears by hand allows the subconscious to process them. Sign off with a statement of release, and if you are spiritual, you can thank your higher power or God here. Ask for calm, clarity, and confidence. Tear up the words afterward; you do not need anyone to read them.

Follow with transcendental meditation, repeating an unloaded word, e.g Om or This This This

Highly recommend seeking out more detail about this top practice with Crappy Childhood Fairy for free at https://courses.crappychildhoodfairy.com/daily-practice

Pattern Interrupters

Taking a cold shower or splashing cold water on your face, suddenly changing posture like standing up quickly, stretching or jumping, tapping alternate sides of the body (bilateral stimulation), or counting down from 100 by sevens can help break the grip of a survival pattern of fight, flight, freeze, or fawn.

Feeling angry or frustrated Stomp your feet, go cycling, punch a pillow, or do some sidekicks to release the pent-up energy in a controlled way.

Feeling scared Hold your hand or place a hand over your heart, "I am safe"

Feeling insecure Stand tall, feet firmly grounded and apart, with your hands on your hips in the Wonder Woman pose. "I am calm and confident"

Feeling small or powerless Stretch your arms wide, reaching skyward.

Expanding your body to create a sense of openness and empowerment.

Say out loud: "I have strength and I am fierce"

Feeling overwhelmed Take a deep breath and forcefully exhale while shaking your arms to release tension and to calm.

Feeling helpless Lift something heavy or engage in a push or pull motion to regain control and capability.

Thought Stops

When you notice negative or anxious thoughts, say "Stop!" out loud or in your mind. Visualize a stop sign or red light and then redirect your thoughts to something positive or neutral.

Dial it down

Imagine you have a dial on your belly, and it's up high to an 8 or 9, then dial it down to a lower number.

Emotional Freedom Technique (EFT) Tapping

Please go to:

https://www.youtube.com/watch?v=XRfLTQjJhp0&t=18s

I use it every time, it can be extremely powerful.

Coregulation is a beautiful thing

Identify safe, supportive people and professionals who are positive in your life. Discuss and be clear about your needs with them before so they understand how to help.

Joining a group meditation or activities like community gardening that prioritize mutual respect are possible safe places.

Being in the presence of a calm person, pet, or even an online guide can have a soothing effect. Hearing their soothing voice, mirroring their relaxed posture, breathing together, a gentle hug, or a reassuring touch on the arm, or cuddling with your pet can all release oxytocin and promote feelings of safety and connection.

At Work or Out and About

Small movements help release tension and refocus your mind, grounding you in the present. Stand, stretch, tense up face, hands or body and release, smile.

Step away to a quieter area, even a restroom, where you can compose yourself away from prying eyes. A few moments of solitude can help you regroup.

Wash your face and hands, feel how good it is!

Drinking can help regulate your breathing and give you a moment to pause.

Identify what's happening and repeat:

I am dysregulating, that's ok, I am safe

Finger Squeeze - each finger from thumb to pinky and back. Swap hands. Focus on the sensation; feeling the skin-to-skin can connect you to the present and interrupt anxious thoughts.

Visualize a calm and safe place, like a beach or a forest. Imagine all the sounds, sights, and smells.

Text or call your safe support if possible. Reach out to someone you trust, even to let them know you feel anxious. Knowing and focusing on someone or a pet who is there for you can be grounding.

Engage your senses by focusing on what you can see, hear, touch, smell, and taste in your immediate environment. Examine your potted plant or photos of a favorite place. Touch a textured object - why I pick up fallen leaves from a walk.

Your Calm Kit

Here are some ideas to prep your personalized toolkit:

in a box or pencil case

a smooth pebble or small object to hold or a crystal

a stress ball

textured fabrics like silk or corduroy

a lovely scented/not scented hand lotion for a self-massage

photos of loved ones or calming nature scenes, a favorite spot to visit

coloring-in book

a doodle book or a book for doodling

a journal with a favorite pen

essential oil like lavender or chamomile (I carry a little vial of Linden flowers that give me memories of a happy place in spring)

a pack of strong mints or gum

a few sachets of your favorite tea

resistance bands for light stretching

an eye mask

a note for yourself reminding you of it getting better and easier

a hard copy of your top strategies

water bottle

noise canceling headphones /earphones

weighted or cozy blanket

Warm lighting

an app that plays calming sounds like ocean waves, rain, or birdsong

a playlist of your favorite music to calm

songs you can move or sing along to

favorite audiobook or podcast or your favorite prompts

guided meditation with mantras, breathing apps eg Headspace, Calm

bilateral recordings or binaural beats or white noise

your supportive contacts - a list of friends, family, or therapists

Crisis Hotline Numbers

Move out of Freeze

With ease-y soothers

Acknowledge that you are in a hypoarousal state and shutting down

Although thoughts are racing your rational brain is going offline

You are not lazy, you have a lot of shxt going on in your mind and body.

That's ok.

Hand on heart, pat and stroke skin to skin if it feels alright, release that oxytocin

I am ok I am safe

I am having an emotional flashback

I am dysregulating

Go coregulate

Connect to the earth, to your body, use your senses

Soothe and move your body

Good posture - holding an open pose, smiling if you can, although it may feel weird or false, will send messages back to your system that you are safe

Walk to a safe place, be in a natural setting, garden

Or walk around the room if that feels safer

Although I am dysregulating right now,
I am safe.

it's not my fault

I am safe

I can handle this

Breath in through your nose and out slower through
an imagined straw

Sway or rock your body

Stretch

Hug yourself

Cuddle a pet

Pat your arms, chest, legs

Message your ear

Message your hands, your neck, the top of your head

Tap on the side of your hands

Tense and release your body

Have a cold shower to shock you into the now

Sing

Hum

drum

Yawn

Chew gum

Eat some protein, porridge, bananas

Drink water

Move move the body

Sweep, clean, garden mindfully

Listen to upbeat music

Play an instrument

Bring your mind to physical sensations with intentional fidgeting eg playing with the feel of the bracelet you are wearing

Cry

Do the Physiological Sigh: Take two quick inhales through the nose, then exhale slowly through the mouth. Repeat this pattern for a few

Resources and References

Written briefly for easy handling. Please fill in the gaps to learn and grow by exploring further.

Developmental Trauma Disorder (DTD) - proposed by Dr. Bessel van der Kolk, focuses on the developmental impact of chronic trauma, mainly occurring during childhood.

Complex or Childhood PTSD / Complex Trauma - resulting from prolonged, repeated exposure to traumatic experiences, e.g abuse and neglect. Characterized by emotional flashbacks, hypervigilance, difficulty maintaining relationships, a negative self-concept, and persistent mistrust of the world.

DTD and CPTSD are not officially recognized in major diagnostic manuals like the DSM-5. This complicates diagnosis and access to robust treatment.

The ACEs / Adverse Childhood Experiences Score, find free tests online

Hölzel, B. K., Carmody, J., Vangel, M., Congleton, C., Yerramsetti, S. M., Gard, T., & Lazar, S. W. (2011). Mindfulness practice leads to increases in regional brain gray matter density. Psychiatry Research: Neuroimaging, 191(1), 36-43.
https://doi.org/10.1016 j.pscychresns.2010.08.006

http://www.youtube.com/@TheTappingSolutionChannel

Anna Runkle (2024) Re-Regulated: Set Your Life Free from Childhood PTSD and the Trauma-Driven Behaviors That Keep You Stuck. Hay House
https://crappychildhoodfairy.com

Bessel van der Kolk (2014) The Body Keeps the Score: Brain, Mind, and Body in the Healing of Trauma. Viking

Emma McAdam is a licensed therapist who offers great practical mental health advice via YouTube
https://www.youtube.com/@TherapyinaNutshell

Judith Herman (1997) Trauma and Recovery: The Aftermath of Violence—From Domestic Abuse to Political Terror. Basic Books

Pete Walker (2013) Complex PTSD: From Surviving to Thriving: A Guide and Map for Recovering from Childhood Trauma. Azure Coyote
I highly recommend his excellent free resources
https://www.pete-walker.com

Richard Grannon, I recommend viewing his:
www.youtube.com/@richardgrannonfortressment9247
and 28 Dec 2020 Master Your Emotions: Identifying Emotional Flashbacks vs Emotions YouTube

Stephanie Foo (2022) What My Bones Know: A Memoir of Healing from Complex Trauma. HarperOne